ER 428.1 CAN
Felix, Rebecca, 1984-
Can you be a bee?

Can You Be a Bee?

FOUNTAINDALE PUBLIC LIBRARY DISTRICT
300 West Briarcliff Road
Bolingbrook, IL 60440-2894
(630) 759-2102

amicus readers

by Rebecca Felix

Ideas for Parents and Teachers

Amicus Readers let children practice reading informational texts at the earliest reading levels. Familiar words and concepts with close photo-text matches support early readers.

Before Reading
- Discuss the cover photo with the child. What does it tell him?
- Ask the child to predict what she will learn in the book.

Read the Book
- "Walk" through the book and look at the photos. Let the child ask questions.
- Read the book to the child, or have the child read independently.

After Reading
- Use the matching quiz at the end of the book to review the text.
- Prompt the child to make connections. Ask: *Can you think of other words that sound the same but have different meanings and spellings?*

Amicus Readers are published by Amicus
P.O. Box 1329, Mankato, MN 56002
www.amicuspublishing.us

Copyright © 2015. International copyright reserved in all countries. No part of this book may be reproduced in any form without written permission from the publisher.

Library of Congress Cataloging-in-Publication Data

Felix, Rebecca, 1984-
  Can you be a bee? / Rebecca Felix.
    pages cm. -- (Hear homophones here)
  Audience: K to Grade 3.
  Audience: Age 6
  ISBN 978-1-60753-569-0 (hardcover) --
  ISBN 978-1-60753-653-6 (pdf ebook)
  1. English language--Homonyms--Juvenile literature.
2. English language--Verb--Juvenile literature. 3. English language--Noun--Juvenile literature. I. Title.
  PE1595.F36 2014
  428'.1--dc 3
                    2013048620

Photo Credits: Shutterstock Images, cover, 1, 3, 5, 10, 15, 16 (top left), 16 (bottom right); Songchai W/Shutterstock Images, 6–7, 16 (middle left); Suja Images/Shutterstock Images, 8, 16 (bottom left); Photastic/Shutterstock Images, 9, 16 (top right); Fuse/Thinkstock, 10–11, 16 (middle right); Monkey Business Images/Thinkstock, 12

Produced for Amicus by The Peterson Publishing Company and Red Line Editorial.

Editor Jenna Gleisner
Designer Jake Nordby
Printed in the United States of America
Mankato, MN
2-2014
PA10001
10 9 8 7 6 5 4 3 2 1

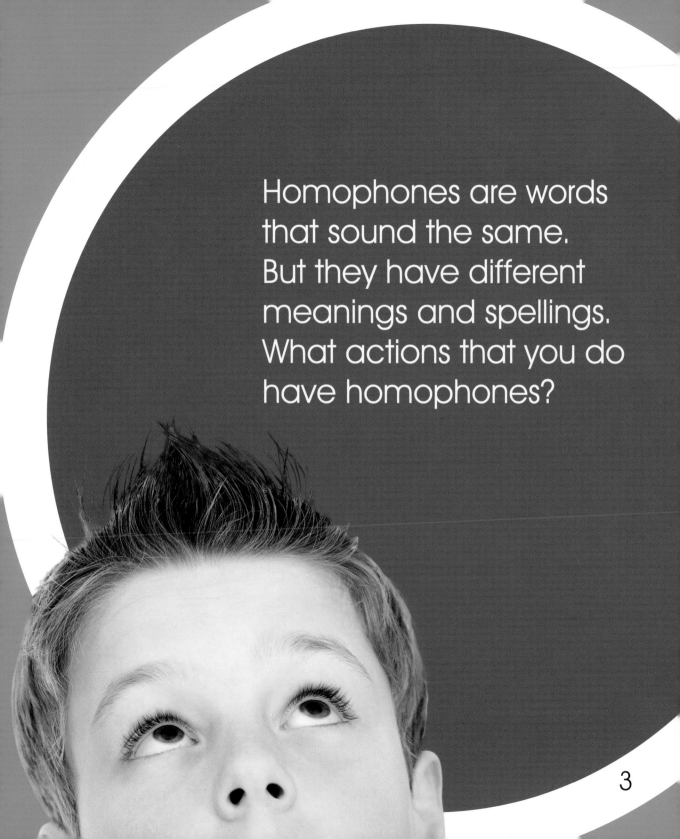

Homophones are words that sound the same. But they have different meanings and spellings. What actions that you do have homophones?

3

be
bee

To **be** means to exist as something. You exist as you. A **bee** is an insect. You cannot **be** a **bee**. But what can you do?

see
sea

To **see** means to look. You can **see** a **sea**. A **sea** is a big body of water with salt in it.

bury
berry

To **bury** means to dig and cover. You can **bury** a **berry**. Just dig a hole and drop in a blueberry.

flee
flea

To **flee** is to run away. You can **flee** from a **flea**. But it might be tough. A **flea** is almost too small to see!

brake
break

To **brake** is to slow down or stop. A **break** is a short pause or rest. You can **brake** your bike to take a **break** at the park.

write right

To **write** is to make letters or numbers on paper. People **write** with either their **right** or left hand. Which hand do you use to **write**?

Match each homophone to its picture!

flee

flea

bury

berry

see

sea

W9-CKI-129

Minnesota

EXPLORE THE UNITED STATES ★ EXPLORE THE UNITED STATES ★ EXPLORE THE UNITED STATES ★ EXPLORE THE UNITED STATES

Julie Murray

Big Buddy BOOKS
Explore the United States

VISIT US AT
www.abdopublishing.com

Published by ABDO Publishing Company, PO Box 398166, Minneapolis, MN 55439.

Copyright © 2013 by Abdo Consulting Group, Inc. International copyrights reserved in all countries. No part of this book may be reproduced in any form without written permission from the publisher. Big Buddy Books™ is a trademark and logo of ABDO Publishing Company.

Printed in the United States of America, North Mankato, Minnesota.
042012
092012

 PRINTED ON RECYCLED PAPER

Coordinating Series Editor: Rochelle Baltzer
Editor: Sarah Tieck
Contributing Editors: Megan M. Gunderson, BreAnn Rumsch, Marcia Zappa
Graphic Design: Adam Craven
Cover Photograph: *Shutterstock*: July Flower.
Interior Photographs/Illustrations: *Alamy*: John Elk III (p. 13); *AP Photo*: Cal Sport Media via AP Images (p. 21), PR NEWSWIRE (p. 19), Alessandro Trovati (p. 25); *Getty Images*: Tom Dahlin (p. 21), Silver Screen Collection/Hulton Archive/Getty Images (p. 23); *iStockphoto*: ©iStockphoto.com/ArtBoyMB (pp. 11, 30), ©iStockphoto.com/BanksPhotos (p. 11), ©iStockphoto.com/jimkrugerjimkruger (p. 9), ©iStockphoto.com/smartstock (p. 19), ©iStockphoto.com/twphotos (p. 17); *Shutterstock*: Gerald A. DeBoer (p. 30), Ffooter (p. 27), fotokik_dot_com (p. 29), Carol Heesen (p. 30), Pete Hoffman (p. 27), Intraclique LLC (p. 26), Phillip Lange (p. 30), mikeledray (p. 26), Sergej Razvodovskij (p. 19), Henryk Sadura (p. 9), Jay Stuhlmiller (p. 27), Wildnerdpix (p. 5).

All population figures taken from the 2010 US census.

Library of Congress Cataloging-in-Publication Data

Murray, Julie, 1969-
 Minnesota / Julie Murray.
   p. cm. -- (Explore the United States)
 ISBN 978-1-61783-361-8
 1. Minnesota--Juvenile literature. I. Title.
 F606.3.M87 2012
 977.6--dc23
                2012007060

Contents

ONE NATION

The United States is a **diverse** country. It has farmland, cities, coasts, and mountains. Its people come from many different backgrounds. And, its history covers more than 200 years.

Today the country includes 50 states. Minnesota is one of these states. Let's learn more about this state and its story!

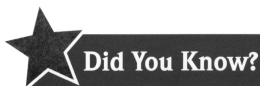

Did You Know?

Minnesota became a state on May 11, 1858. It was the thirty-second state to join the nation.

4

Minnesota

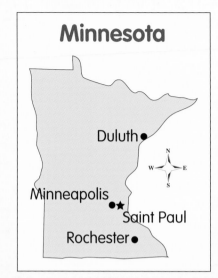

- Duluth
- Minneapolis
- Saint Paul
- Rochester

N W E S

The Minnesota State Capitol opened in 1905.

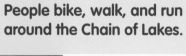

People bike, walk, and run around the Chain of Lakes.

9

Minnesota's third-largest city is Rochester. It is home to 106,769 people. The Mayo Clinic is located there. This is a world-famous medical center.

Duluth is the state's fourth-largest city, with 86,265 people. It is a port city on Lake Superior. Ships from around the world travel to Duluth.

The Mayo Clinic is in downtown Rochester.

Duluth has a bridge that lifts so large ships can pass into its harbor.

11

MINNESOTA IN HISTORY

Minnesota's history includes Native Americans and settlers. By 1660, the first French explorers had come to Minnesota from Lake Superior. They met Native Americans who had lived there for many years. Soon, fur traders started visiting the area.

In 1819, a **fort** was built in present-day Minneapolis. It became known as Fort Snelling. It helped keep peace on the unsettled land. Over time, **missionaries** and settlers arrived. Minnesota became a state in 1858.

In the 1700s, Grand Portage was a major fur-trading center. Today, visitors can see what life was like during that time.

Timeline

1803

President Thomas Jefferson arranged for the United States to buy land in the **Louisiana Purchase**. It included part of present-day Minnesota.

1886

Saint Paul held its first Winter Carnival. It is the oldest and largest winter carnival in the United States.

1800s

Minnesota became the thirty-second state on May 11.

1858

Doctors in the Mayo family began treating people. This was the start of the Mayo Clinic in Rochester.

1889

1927

Charles Lindbergh, who grew up in Little Falls, flew across the Atlantic Ocean. He was the first person to do this alone and without stopping.

1956

Southdale Center opened in Edina. It was the first US indoor shopping mall.

1992

The Mall of America opened in Bloomington. It was the largest US indoor shopping mall.

2010

The Minnesota Twins baseball team got a new stadium in Minneapolis called Target Field.

1900s

2000s

Minnesota senator Hubert H. Humphrey became US vice president. He served with President Lyndon B. Johnson.

Minnesota senator Walter Mondale became US vice president. He served with President Jimmy Carter.

In Minneapolis, a major bridge across the Mississippi River collapsed. This caused many injuries and deaths.

1965

1977

2007

15

ACROSS THE LAND

Minnesota has forests, hills, rivers, and lakes. Water covers about 4,780 square miles (12,380 sq km) of the state. The Mississippi River starts in northern Minnesota. And, the state borders part of Lake Superior.

Many types of animals make their homes in Minnesota. These include deer, rabbits, and gophers. Beavers and loons live in the state's waters.

Did You Know?

In July, the average temperature in Minnesota is 70°F (21°C). In January, it is 8°F (-13°C).

Split Rock Lighthouse overlooks Lake Superior.

EARNING A LIVING

Minnesota has many businesses. Some of them make food products, such as flour and butter. Others make **technology** and **electronics**. Also, many people work in finance, health care, and education.

Minnesota farms grow corn, soybeans, wheat, and apples. Some produce dairy and livestock.

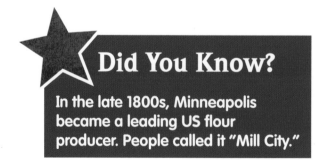

Did You Know?

In the late 1800s, Minneapolis became a leading US flour producer. People called it "Mill City."

General Mills, Land O'Lakes, and 3M are Minnesota companies. They make products such as cereals, milk, and tape.

19

SPORTS PAGE

Minnesota is home to many **professional** sports teams. These include baseball, football, basketball, and hockey teams. The state also has popular college sports teams, including the University of Minnesota Gophers.

Outdoor sports are popular in Minnesota, too. Many people enjoy fishing, hunting, boating, ice skating, and skiing.

Did You Know?

Minnesota is sometimes called "the State of Hockey."

The Minnesota Wild play hockey in Saint Paul.

The University of Minnesota Gophers play football at TCF Bank Stadium in Minneapolis.

HOMETOWN HEROES

Many famous people are from Minnesota. Judy Garland was born in Grand Rapids in 1922. Her real name was Frances Gumm. She was an actress and singer. She starred in many movies.

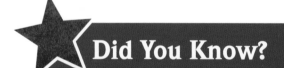

Did You Know?

Today, people can see Garland's childhood home in Grand Rapids. It has been made into the Judy Garland Museum.

Garland (*center*) played Dorothy in the 1939 movie *The Wizard of Oz.*

BELL
OUT OF ORDER
PLEASE KNOCK

Lindsey Kildow Vonn was born in Saint Paul in 1984. She is one of the world's best skiers!

Vonn has more World Cup **titles** than any other American skier. And in 2010, she became the first American woman to win an Olympic gold medal in the downhill event.

Vonn learned to ski at Buck Hill in Burnsville.
It is near the home she grew up in.

25

Tour Book

Do you want to go to Minnesota? If you visit the state, here are some places to go and things to do!

 ## Explore

Vacation in Brainerd in central Minnesota. There, you can swim, bike, and boat in the summer. Many people ice fish there in the winter.

 ## Taste

Try some food on a stick at the Minnesota State Fair! That is what this famous Saint Paul event is known for. The fair starts every year at the end of August.

 Cheer

Watch the Minnesota Twins play baseball at Target Field! Minnesota native Joe Mauer became the team's catcher in 2004.

Remember

See some of the state's oldest buildings at Fort Snelling in Minneapolis. Workers in costumes talk about the fort's history.

Discover

Visit Itasca State Park to camp and hike. Lake Itasca is famous because it is where the Mississippi River starts.

A Great State

The story of Minnesota is important to the United States. The people and places that make up this state offer something special to the country. Together with all the states, Minnesota helps make the United States great.

Downtown Minneapolis has a popular riverfront area.
It includes parks, restaurants, theaters, and a museum.

29

Fast Facts

Date of Statehood:
May 11, 1858

Population (rank):
5,303,925
(21st most-populated state)

Total Area (rank):
86,935 square miles
(12th largest state)

Motto:
"L'Étoile du Nord"
(The Star of the North)

Nickname:
North Star State,
Gopher State,
Land of 10,000 Lakes

State Capital:
Saint Paul

Flag:

Flower: Pink-and-White Lady's Slipper

Postal Abbreviation:
MN

Tree: Red, or Norway, Pine

Bird: Common Loon

Important Words

capital a city where government leaders meet.
diverse made up of things that are different from each other.
electronics products that work by controlling the flow of electricity. These often do useful things.
fort a building with strong walls to guard against enemies.
Louisiana Purchase land the United States purchased from France in 1803. It extended from the Mississippi River to the Rocky Mountains and from Canada through the Gulf of Mexico.
missionary a person who travels to share his or her religious beliefs with others.
professional (pruh-FEHSH-nuhl) working for money rather than for pleasure.
region a large part of a country that is different from other parts.
technology (tehk-NAH-luh-jee) the use of science for practical purposes.
title a first-place position in a contest.

Web Sites

To learn more about Minnesota, visit ABDO Publishing Company online. Web sites about Minnesota are featured on our Book Links page. These links are routinely monitored and updated to provide the most current information available.

www.abdopublishing.com

Index